PROJECT

CODE

CREATE AN ANIMATION
WITH SCRATCH

Illustrated by
Glen McBeth

Kevin Wood

Lerner Publications ◆ Minneapolis

First American edition published in 2018 by Lerner Publishing Group, Inc.

First published in Great Britain in 2017 by
The Watts Publishing Group, an imprint of Hachette Children's Group

Speech bubble designed by Freepik
Main body text set in Neo Sans Std 13/20.
Typeface provided by Monotype Typography.

Library of Congress Cataloging-in-Publication Data

The Cataloging-in-Publication Data for *Create an Animation with Scratch*
    is on file at the Library of Congress.
ISBN 978-1-5415-2436-1 (lib. bdg.)
ISBN 978-1-5415-2513-9 (pbk.)
ISBN 978-1-5415-2441-5 (EB pdf)

Printed in China

Lerner Publications Company
A division of Lerner Publishing Group, Inc.
241 First Avenue North
Minneapolis, MN 55401 USA

For reading levels and more information, look up this title at
www.lernerbooks.com.

MIX
Paper from
responsible sources
FSC
www.fsc.org
FSC® C104740

Using Scratch

Scratch is a programming language designed by MIT (Massachusetts Institute of Technology) that
lets you create your own interactive stories, animations, games, music, and art. Rather than using
a complex computer language, it uses easy-to-understand coding blocks. To get the most out of
this book, you will need to be able to use a computer and you will need to load Scratch onto your
computer. Always check with an adult if it is OK to download files from the Internet to your computer.
Go to: **https://scratch.mit.edu**.

First, do Scratch's "Getting Started with Scratch" tutorial, found by going to "Create" on the home
page, and then look in the "Tips" menu. You can also work on Scratch off-line. Scroll to the
bottom of the home page and click on Offline Editor in the Support menu. Follow the
instructions to install it on your computer.

CONTENTS

To load the projects that you will use in this book, go to:

www.lernerbooks.com/go/project-code-download

and select "Animation." Save the folder somewhere on your computer where you will be able to find it again. You will need to open files in this folder as you go through the project.

Every effort has been made by the Publishers to ensure that the websites in this book are suitable for children, that they are of the highest educational value, and that they contain no inappropriate or offensive material. However, because of the nature of the Internet, it is impossible to guarantee that the contents of these sites will not be altered. We strongly advise that Internet access is supervised by a responsible adult.

ALL ABOUT ANIMATION

>>> Animation is a technique where a series of drawings appear to move when they are shown quickly, one after the other. It's fun to watch animated films and cartoons, but have you ever wanted to create your own animation? >>>

Animated films can take years to make and need hundreds of **animators** to create thousands of images. Most modern animation films use computers and **code** to create these images and most animators start out by learning animation skills on a home computer.

Flip books

Have you ever seen or made a flip book? A flip book (or flick book) is a book with a series of pictures that are slightly different on each page. The pictures are usually drawn near the bottom right corner of the book. If you flick through them quickly, using your thumb, it looks as though the picture is moving.

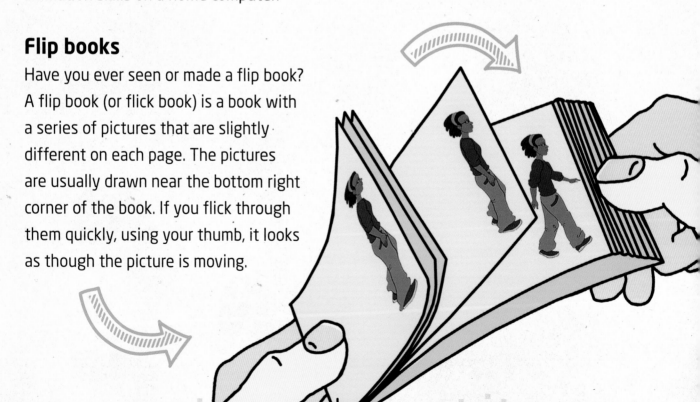

Easy animation

In a notebook, draw a stick man standing, then gradually bending his knees, then straightening them again, then rising into the air. Use a new page for each illustration. When the pages are flicked, it will look as if the stick man is crouching and then jumping into the air. That's how animation works.

Starting from Scratch

Scratch helps you create fun animations easily. Using already-written pieces of code that you can download, the projects in this book will let you play with the code and understand more about how coding works.

You don't need to be good at drawing to use Scratch. **Sprites**, backgrounds, and **costumes** are all on the site, ready to use. This means you can create animations much faster on a computer than you can by hand, and you can change things more easily too with the click of a mouse!

Think about it

Can you think of other ways that you could create an animation without using drawings or a computer? How do you think the *Wallace and Gromit* films were made?

(answer on page 32)

You can use the skills you'll learn from interacting with the animation projects in this book to develop animations of your own. Once you've gotten the hang of the basics, the possibilities to be creative are endless!

CODE AND BINARY

>>> Computers do exactly what they are told to do. They cannot guess what you want them to do. They receive step-by-step instructions from computer **programs** that are written in code. Code is made up of clear, **logical** instructions that use a simple system called binary. Binary means "something that is made up of two things."

Binary

Think of binary as being a little like a light switch. It has only two instructions—"on" and "off." Computers read binary using just two numbers: 1 and 0.

1 = on
0 = off

Computers read binary instructions (a bit like we read the letters that make up words and sentences) to work out what the code in the program is telling it to do. It's surprising how much information you can give a computer using only these two numbers.

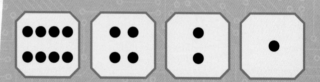

Using these four cards and binary, you can write any number from 0-15.

   a "1" means the card is face up (on).
   a "0" means the card is face down (off).

Add up all the dots on the cards below that have a 1 underneath them.

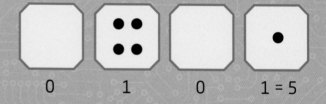

0   1   0   1 = 5

Can you work out the answer to the one below? (answer on page 32)

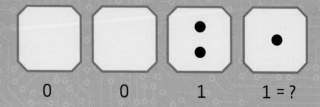

0   0   1   1 = ?

Coding unplugged

Try this activity to see if you can write clear coding instructions.
You will need: a partner, a pen and paper, and objects to use as obstacles.

1 Make a simple obstacle course. You could put some cushions on the floor or draw sharks on some paper and place them on the ground.

2 Your aim is to get your partner from one end of the course to the other. Write your instructions using this code and put a comma between each instruction.

↑ = move forward one step

⟶ = sidestep right one step

⟵ = sidestep left one step

3 Ask your partner to follow your code to navigate the obstacles safely. Did the code work?

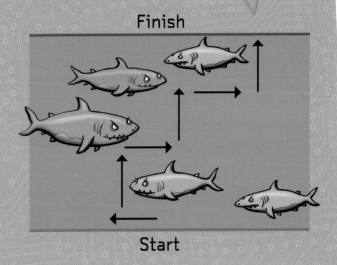

Finish

Start

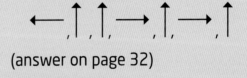

The code below for the shark obstacle course has a mistake in it. Can you find it?

⟵ ,↑ ,↑ ,⟶ ,↑ ,⟶ ,↑

(answer on page 32)

Do I need to know binary to use Scratch?

No. Scratch is a coding tool that **translates** binary instructions into user-friendly blocks of code. **Users** simply drag and drop, and join together the blocks to make programs. Explore the tutorials in the "Scratch Tips" menu to practice using the blocks.

Think about it

Can you understand this well-known computer joke?

"There are 10 types of people in the world. Those who understand binary and those who don't!"

ALL ABOUT LOOPS

A computer will **run** the instructions in a code, one after the other, from beginning to end and then stop. If you want a computer to repeat the same thing over and over again, you need to use a type of code called a loop.

Step to it

If you wanted to tell your friend to take 10 steps across the room, you wouldn't say "take a step, take a step, take a step . . ." ten times! You would say "take 10 steps." You do exactly the same when you're coding.

And repeat

The repeat bit of the code is a loop. This is also called "going around the loop" or "an **iteration**," which means that we run the code from top to bottom each time we go around the loop.

It's much easier and quicker to write a looping code because it is shorter. It's easier to make changes to it, too.

Instead of writing the code:	It is better to write the code:
MOVE 1 step	REPEAT 10 times:
WAIT 0.5 seconds	MOVE 1 step
MOVE 1 step	WAIT 0.5 secs
WAIT 0.5 seconds	
MOVE 1 step	
WAIT 0.5 seconds	
. . . and so on, seven more times . . .	

Think about it

If you told your friend to "take a step, take a step," ten times, it would take much longer for them to cross the room than if you'd said "take ten steps," as they'd have to wait for each individual "take a step" instruction.

Make coding quicker with subroutines

Code that is used more than once can be made into a subroutine. You write some code and give it a name, then simply add this name to your main code each time you want to use the subroutine.

Scratch lets you make blocks of your own code. To make a simple subroutine in Scratch, click on the "More Blocks" tab and click "Make a Block." Name the block: STEP
Next, add these blocks from the colored menu tabs:

MOVE 1 step
WAIT 0.5 secs

To use the STEP subroutine in your code, put your STEP block inside a repeat loop as shown.

move 10 step
wait 0.5 secs

STEP

Nested loops

You can use a loop inside another loop. This is called a "nested loop." Try acting out this nested loop. Face an object, and then turn 90 degrees to the right four times. You have performed a loop. Now clap each time your feet move. The clap is the nested loop.

Try out your new loop skills in the Scratch project on the next page.

GET LOOPING!

>>> For the animation project, we will start by creating a simple animation of a sprite, named Avery, walking. Open the Scratch project "animation1.sb2."

 Click on "Costumes" to see four different images. Each shows Avery at a different stage of walking. Showing these images one after the other will animate Avery walking.

2 To do this, we have created a simple loop. A "forever" loop does exactly what it says—it runs the code inside it over and over again, forever. This code changes to the next costume, moves forward a little, waits for 0.2 seconds, and then repeats. But if you run this code by clicking on it, Avery will eventually walk off the screen.

3 We can fix this by using repeat loops "nested" inside a forever loop. The top repeat loop walks Avery halfway across the screen. The "point in direction" block turns her around. The bottom repeat loop walks Avery back again and then turns her around. She will do this forever or until you stop her.

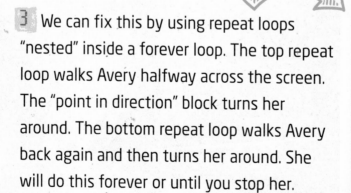

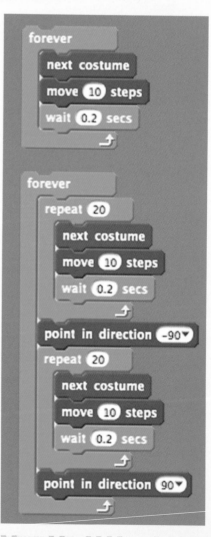

```
forever
    next costume
    move 10 steps
    wait 0.2 secs
```

```
forever
    repeat 20
        next costume
        move 10 steps
        wait 0.2 secs
    point in direction -90▾
    repeat 20
        next costume
        move 10 steps
        wait 0.2 secs
    point in direction 90▾
```

4 As we are using the same code twice, we've created a "walk" subroutine.

Note that a drumbeat has been added to the subroutine. By putting a repeat loop inside a repeat loop, Avery's costume changes twice for each drumbeat. This way you hear a drumbeat each time her foot touches the ground.

AHA!

Using a subroutine not only saves space and time, it makes code much more readable!

5 Use the "Walk" subroutine block in your final code. Click on this piece of code in the project.

Three more blocks set where Avery starts walking from. These blocks place her at a point to the bottom left of the screen, facing to the right, and also set the volume of the drumbeat sound.

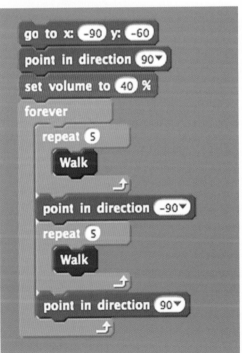

CREATE A CHARACTER

>>> You can have fun making a Scratch animation exactly how you want it. There are many different sprites to choose from as your main character. Open a new Scratch project by clicking on "File," then "New" in the dropdown menu. Choose sprites from the Scratch library by clicking on the sprite image next to the words "New sprite."

Get creative

If you don't like any of those, you can create your own! Choose the paintbrush tool from the "New sprite" menu and a blank page will appear. Use the paintbrush or shapes, such as the line, rectangle, and circle, to create your sprite. Choose colors from the menu at the bottom and use the slider to change the size of your paintbrush. Create more than one costume (position) for your sprite by clicking on the "paint new costume" paintbrush tool.

Snap!

Click on the icon of a file and you can add any image you have saved on your computer as a sprite, too. Most picture formats can be used, such as JPEG and PNG files.

If you prefer, you can add a photo of yourself! Click on the camera and if your computer has a camera you will see a picture of yourself come up on the screen!

Storyboards

Think of some animated films you have seen. What did you like about them? Was it the characters, the story, or both? Most good animations have interesting characters and an exciting storyline that makes you want to see what happens next.

When animators start creating an animation, they first make a storyboard. This is a rough outline of what will happen to the characters in a film or animation. It is usually a series of drawings that map out the key moments or events in a story. It helps an animator to get a clear idea of the story's beginning, middle, and end before they start. Try it with a character you have created.

DECISIONS, DECISIONS!

>>> Decisions are an important part of coding. Decisions mean a computer can make choices based on what is happening. The computer's ability to make decisions makes it seem intelligent, but in reality it is simply following a logical set of instructions.

How do decisions work?

You can create many types of decision in coding, but they all follow the same basic format:

DECISION   CONDITION   ACTION

This may sound confusing, but it is easy really. You probably use the words IF, WHEN, or WHILE every day, and they have the same meaning in code as they do in real life. IF you are hungry, what should you do?

In coding, the **CONDITION** is what you are testing for. The CONDITION must always be either true or false. So if you are testing to see IF you are hungry, then . . .

yes = true
no = false

The ACTION part is what you do if the CONDITION is true. So IF you are hungry, the ACTION is that you will eat.

What else?

The simplest of decisions is the IF statement. This usually includes a THEN part. For example, the coder can tell the computer, "IF this happens, THEN do this." Sometimes an ELSE part is also added. This allows the coder to tell the computer, "IF this happens, THEN do this or ELSE do that." For example:

IF hungry, THEN eat or ELSE keep playing.

The IF-THEN-ELSE game

Try this game with some friends. One person is the Coder, everyone else is a Computer. The Coder gives a command.
"IF I _____ (do this),
THEN you _____ (do this)."
An example might be: "IF I pat my head, THEN you hop on one leg."

Now try an IF-THEN-ELSE statement.
"IF I _____ (do this),
THEN you _____ (do this),
or ELSE you _____ (do that)."
An example might be: "IF I pat my head, THEN you hop on one leg, or ELSE stick your tongue out." If the Coder does nothing, the Computers should all stick their tongues out!

Try coding using decisions in Scratch on the next page.

USING DECISIONS

>>> Adding decisions to our project will make it more intelligent. Open the Scratch project named "animation2.sb2."

1 The first decision to add is a "when" statement at the start of the code. This tells the computer: "When I click on the green flag, start the animation." (The green start flag and red stop buttons are at the top right of the Scratch project screen.)

2 The next decision adds a little more intelligence to Avery's walking. At the moment she walks back and forth a set number of paces. We have made it more intelligent by sensing when Avery reaches the edge of the screen, using a block of IF code.

This block makes Avery walk a few paces and then check if she has reached the edge. IF she has, the code turns her around.

3 Make another subroutine called JUMP.

Changing the "Y" value makes Avery move up and down. The first "change" block moves her up 60 "steps" and the second 60 steps back down again, with a small delay in between.

4 Note that there is a red mark on the path. If the computer senses that Avery is touching the red mark, the CONDITION (IF touching color red?) is met (true). The computer then runs the code for the IF-THEN statement with the JUMP subroutine and Avery will jump in the air.

5 We can also make Avery do something if the condition was not met, or false. This tells the computer, "IF Avery is touching the red, THEN think nothing and jump, or ELSE think 'Hmmm.'"

6 Now, when you click the green flag, Avery walks across the screen, thinking "Hmmm." She turns around at the edges of the screen. Whenever she touches the red mark, she thinks nothing and jumps up and down four times. This continues until you click on the stop **symbol**.

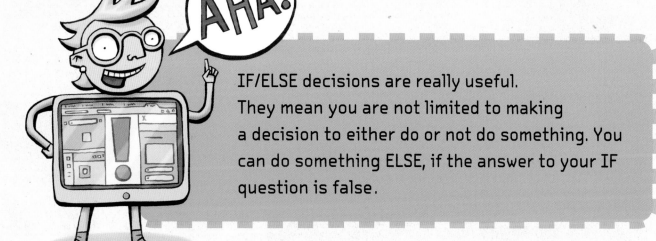

IF/ELSE decisions are really useful. They mean you are not limited to making a decision to either do or not do something. You can do something ELSE, if the answer to your IF question is false.

WHAT'S AN OPERATOR?

Data is any collection of information, such as numbers or measurements. Different types of operators control how the computer uses the data.

Some math operators are:
add +, subtract -,
multiply x, and divide ÷

Some comparison operators are:
less than <, greater than >,
and equal to =

Logic operators are:
AND, OR, and NOT

AND logic

AND logic tests to see if the answer to more than one question is true. For example: IF hungry AND lunchtime, THEN eat.

Each condition (question) is still either true or false, but the result of the combined test—whether we are hungry AND it is lunchtime—is also either true or false.

Logic operators

The answer to "am I hungry?" is either "yes" (true) or "no" (false). What if you wanted to know "am I hungry and is it lunchtime?" Logic operators are used in coding because they test for more than one thing at a time, using the words AND and OR.

The AND logic works like this:
Hungry (true) AND lunchtime (true)
= true (eat)
Hungry (true) AND NOT lunchtime (false)
= false (don't eat)
NOT hungry (false) AND lunchtime (true)
= false (don't eat)
NOT hungry (false) AND NOT
lunchtime (false)
= false (don't eat)

OR logic

OR logic tests to see if only *one* of the conditions is true. For example:
IF I am Tired OR it is Dark, THEN go indoors.

The OR logic works like this:
Tired (true) OR dark (true) = true (go indoors)
Tired (true) OR NOT dark (false) = true (go indoors)
NOT tired (false) OR dark (true) = true (go indoors)
NOT tired (false) OR NOT dark (false) = false (don't go indoors)

So if *either* of our conditions is true, the whole test is true. The test would only be false if you are not tired and it is not dark.

Conditional operators

Conditional operators let us ask more complicated questions. You may want to know *how* hungry you are. If you were a little hungry you would eat an apple. If you were very hungry you would eat a meal. For these questions, we use the > or < symbols, which show that one side is bigger than the other.
4 > 2 means 4 is greater than 2
2 < 4 means 2 is less than 4

You can say how hungry you are using a scale of 1 to 10.
If 1 = not hungry and 10 = starving, then you can say:
IF hungry > 7 THEN eat lunch
IF hungry < 3 THEN carry on playing
IF hungry > 3 AND hungry < 7 THEN eat an apple

Think about it

When someone next asks you if you are hungry, try to answer them using greater than or less than and a scale of 1 to 10.

ADDING OPERATORS

>>> So far we have only asked simple questions in our code, such as "are we touching the red spot?" or "have we reached the edge of the screen?" When we need to ask more specific questions, we need to use operator blocks. Open the Scratch project named "animation3.sb2."

1 Avery jumps when she walks past the red mark in either direction. If we only wanted her to jump when moving to the right, we need to use two operators, AND and =. Both of these conditions—touching the red mark and a travel direction of 90 (right)—must now be met before she will jump.

2 A third decision uses =, >, and <, and two AND operators. Remember ">" means greater than and "<" means less than. This time, when Avery is walking to the right AND her position on the screen is between 1 and 40 (just over halfway) Avery will do a somersault. Like the jump, the somersault is a subroutine.

3 The somersault subroutine looks complicated, but here's how it works. To turn a circle Avery has to **rotate** 360 degrees. This block moves Avery 15 degrees at a time to make the animation smooth as she goes around.

360 ÷ 15 = 24, so to complete a circle, the block repeats moving 15 degrees 24 times: 12 for the first 180 degrees and 12 for the remaining 180 degrees.

The first "set rotation style" block tells the computer that we want to rotate rather than turn around. The second "set rotation style" block tells Avery to turn around at the edge of the screen.

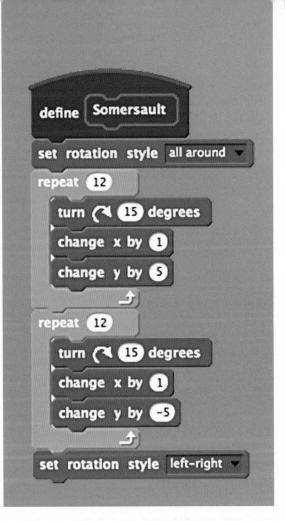

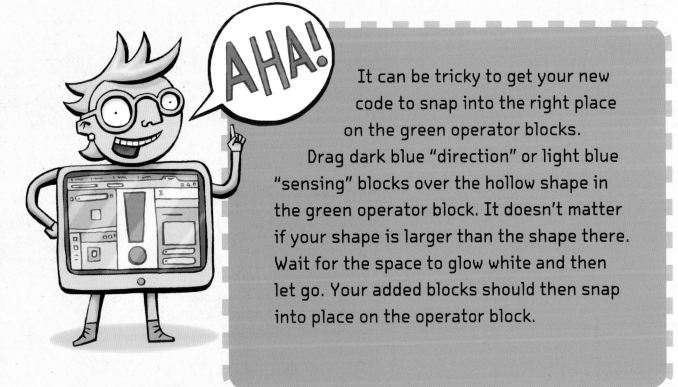

AHA!

It can be tricky to get your new code to snap into the right place on the green operator blocks. Drag dark blue "direction" or light blue "sensing" blocks over the hollow shape in the green operator block. It doesn't matter if your shape is larger than the shape there. Wait for the space to glow white and then let go. Your added blocks should then snap into place on the operator block.

MAKE FUN BACKDROPS

Characters and action are important in animation, but the background plays a big part in bringing it all to life. As with the sprites (see pages 12-13) you can get creative making your own backgrounds. Either choose a background (called "Backdrops" in Scratch) from the Backdrop Library, paint your own background using the creative tools, select a background that you already have on file on your computer, or click on the camera and see what your computer is seeing.

It's behind you!

Different settings really change the mood of your animation. Think about what kind of background will fit with the story of your animation. An underwater background won't fit with a story set in a forest. A really crazy animation might need you to make a funky background to go with it if there's nothing suitable in the library.

Changing colors

One simple way to jazz up your background is to make it change color every few seconds. That can look pretty cool.

Here's the code that you need to make this happen:

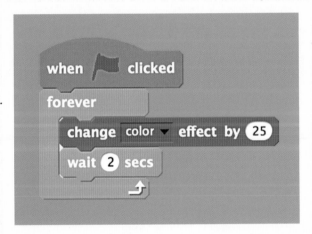

```
when  [flag]  clicked
forever
    change  color ▼  effect by  25
    wait  2  secs
```

1 To apply the code to your background, first, select your background, and then click on "Scripts."

2 Select the blocks you need from the "Events," "Control," and "Looks" menus. Drag these blocks into place, as shown above.

3 When you click the green flag, the background color will change every two seconds. You can alter how quickly it changes color by adjusting the number in the "wait 2 secs" box. Try it on different backgrounds and see which one you like the best.

23

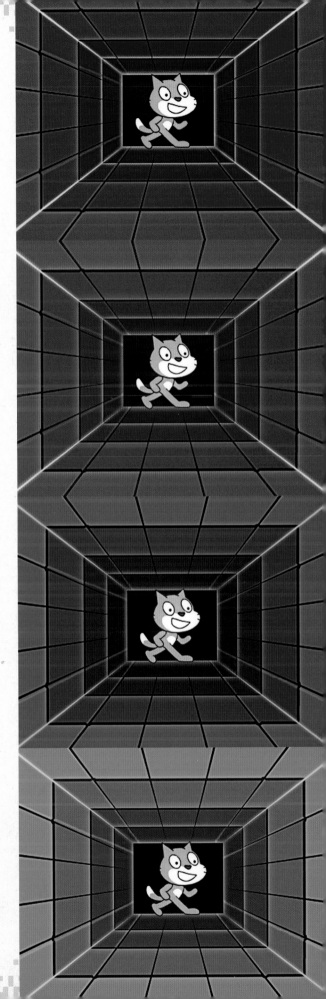

PEOPLE POWER!

>>> Some computer programs need a user (you) to interact with them, such as when you are playing a computer game. Other programs, such as an **operating system**, run without a user having to do anything.

Inputs and outputs

Most programs do interact with a user— a game would not be much fun if you couldn't control what was going on! These interactions fall into two main sections: input and output. Inputs are when the user gives information or instruction to the code, and outputs are when the code responds to the user in some way.

The most obvious inputs are the keyboard and mouse, or the touch screen on a handheld device. When you use them, you give the program information.

The most obvious output is the display screen, where your code displays messages, graphics, or pictures, or it plays a video or music.

Think about it

Do you think the following are inputs or outputs?
• typing your name
• displaying a message on-screen
• printing a picture
• swiping a touch screen
(answers on page 32)

Interface

The connection between a user and a computer is called a UI (User Interface) or GUI (Graphic User Interface). For most programs, user interaction is vital.

Events

If your code needs information from a user, it will usually do one of two things. Either it may ask a question on-screen and wait for an answer or the code will carry on running and respond when the user decides to interact with it. We call this being "event-driven." An "event" might be clicking a mouse or pressing a key.

Think like a computer

Think of the things that you could do in an animation. How do you want your program to react to each of them? Maybe you could write some code like this:

IF up arrow key pressed THEN (computer thinks: *"Which key was pressed? Was it an arrow key? Do I need to move the sprite up?"*)

IF sound menu selected THEN (computer thinks: *"Find which sound command was selected and respond."*)

IF mouse clicked THEN (computer thinks: *"Where was the mouse clicked? What object was selected? Do I need to respond?"*)

IF nothing happens THEN (computer thinks: *"Continue doing what I was already doing."*)

Try adding some user interaction to your code on the next page.

PROJECT PAGE:
USER INTERACTION

>>> Now to add some user interaction. Open the Scratch project named "animation4.sb2."

There are now two sprites—Avery and a bat. Avery will walk back and forth until you tell her to do something else. We've also added a spooky, whirling forest background using the same method as the color changing background on page 23, but by choosing "whirl" from the menu instead of "color."

1 Avery might be a bit scared by the spooky forest. You can get her to jump up and down using this piece of code (right). Hold the mouse button down until she jumps. The "IF mouse down? THEN" block asks the computer to look for a user interaction to see if the mouse has been clicked.

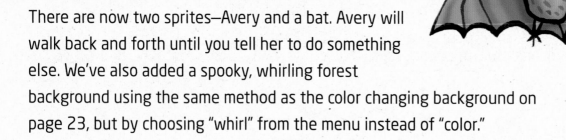

2 You can get Avery to turn a somersault or leap by using this code and holding down the up arrow key on your keyboard.

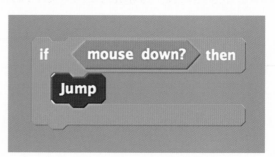

3 You can't see the bat sprite, but if you press the space bar, the bat flies from the top of the screen. If the bat hits Avery, it says "Ouch" and you hear a popping sound. If the bat misses, it disappears.

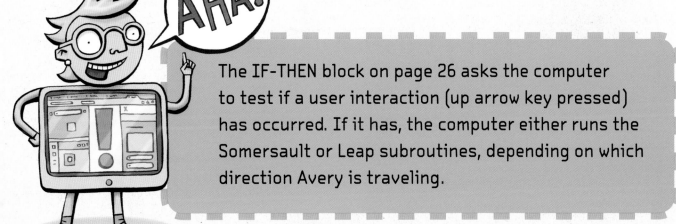

The IF-THEN block on page 26 asks the computer to test if a user interaction (up arrow key pressed) has occurred. If it has, the computer either runs the Somersault or Leap subroutines, depending on which direction Avery is traveling.

4 Click on the bat sprite to see how the code that makes it interact with Avery is made.

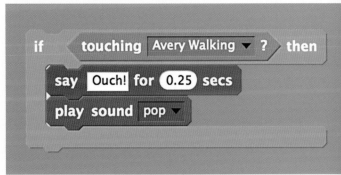

Ouch!

This IF-THEN block of code asks the computer to test if the bat touches Avery. If it does, it runs the code. But it also depends on user interaction to make it work. If the user mistimes hitting the space bar, the IF-THEN part of the code won't run.

5 Click the green flag to start the finished animation. Animate the bat by hitting the space bar. See if you can time animating the bat so it says "Ouch." Try pressing combinations of keys to see all the animation in action.

DEBUGGING

>>> You might think that every time you use the coding blocks, they will do exactly what you wanted, in exactly the way you intended the very first time. Unfortunately, this is rare!

Stop bugging me!

You will probably get something wrong, or the code won't do exactly what you expected. It is not always your fault. Sometimes the program that we use to create the code has a problem, which means that it produces the wrong code.

When code has a problem this is called a bug. Debugging is when you look through the code to see what is causing the bug and fix it by removing the bug.

Before you give code you have written to someone else to use, you should test it. Does it do everything correctly? What if the user does something unexpected? Does our code then have a problem, or does it still work?

AHA!

Why "bug"? Some people think that the term was invented in 1947 when a butterfly was found in an early computer, called Mark II, at Harvard University. The word had also been used by people working with electrical systems. It is said to be short for "bugbear" or "bugaboo," which are old words for an imaginary evil goblin.

Bug hunt

The hardest part of debugging is finding the piece of code that is wrong. You have to look through the code very carefully to see where the bug is. You then have to be careful that any changes made do not cause another bug.

Once the bug is fixed, test the code again until you are sure everything works as it should. Only then is your code finished.

Load the project named "animation5.sb2." Can you spot the bug in this bit of code? Avery is supposed to walk backward and forward. Run this code in Scratch and see what happens. Then try to debug the code and make Avery walk across the screen, like she does in the first project on page 10.
(answer on page 32)

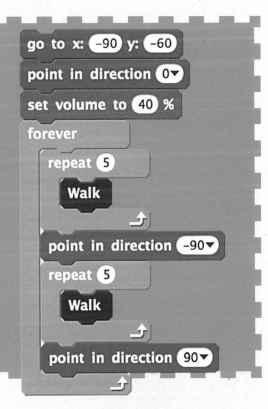

Making mistakes

Remember, debugging is part of coding, and making mistakes is an important part of learning new skills. Sometimes mistakes make unexpected or fun things happen, which you might decide to keep in another animation.

Now, use the skills you have learned to make an animation of your own. The possibilities are endless!

29

GLOSSARY

animator A person who makes an animated cartoon.

code A set of instructions for a computer.

condition A condition is when a computer program examines whether a statement is true or false.

costumes In Scratch, these are the different positions each sprite is drawn in, which give the illusion of animation when they are shown one after the other.

iteration A process used by computers, in which a series of operations is repeated a number of times.

logical Something that follows the rules of logic, or reasoning.

operating system The main program in a computer that controls the way the computer works and makes it possible for other programs to function.

program A set of step-by-step instructions that tell a computer to do something with data.

rotate To turn or cause to turn about an axis or a center.

run To operate.

sprite A simple, two-dimensional bitmap character that can be moved around within a larger scene.

symbol A letter, character, or sign used instead of a word or group of words.

translate To change words or other instructions from one language to another.

user The person who is operating the computer program.

MORE INFORMATION

BOOKS

Breen, Derek. *Creating Digital Animations: Animate Stories with Scratch! (Dummies Junior).* New York: John Wiley & Sons, 2016.

Gifford, Clive. *Get Ahead in Computing: Computing and Coding in the Real World.* London: Wayland, 2017.

Vorderman, Carol. *Coding With Scratch Made Easy.* London: DK Children, 2015.

Wainewright, Max. *Generation Code: I'm an Advanced Scratch Coder.* London: Wayland, 2017.

WEBSITES

MIT's Scratch website, where you can download the program for free
https://scratch.mit.edu/about/

Kidzsearch website with information about animation and useful links
http://wiki.kidzsearch.com/wiki/Animation

VISIT

The **Walt Disney Family Museum**, San Francisco, California, has activities, events, and classes for families and kids. Explore the history of Walt Disney, and learn how animators brought drawings and objects to life. Check out this museum, and look for other museums and computer coding classes in your area.

INDEX

ANSWERS

page 5 The *Wallace and Gromit* films are made using a technique called "stop motion." Clay models are used and the film is recorded one frame, or picture, at a time. The model is moved a tiny amount for each frame, so that when the frames are run as a sequence, the model looks like it is moving.

page 6 Binary cards 0011 = 3

page 7 The mistake in the shark obstacle course is the third instruction (the second up arrow).

page 24 Typing your name and swiping a touchscreen are inputs. Displaying a message and printing a picture are outputs.

page 29 The bug is the first "point in direction" block. It should be 90, rather than 0.